Fact Finders®

Amazing Animal Colonies

TERMITES
Secrets of Their Cozy Colonies

by Rebecca Stefoff

Consultant:
Matthew Bertone, PhD
Entomologist
Plant Disease & Insect Clinic
North Carolina State University

CAPSTONE PRESS
a capstone imprint

Fact Finders Books are published by Capstone Press,
1710 Roe Crest Drive, North Mankato, Minnesota 56003
www.mycapstone.com

Library of Congress Cataloging-in-Publication Data
Names: Stefoff, Rebecca, 1951- author.
Title: Termites : secrets of their cozy colonies / by Rebecca Stefoff.
Description: North Mankato, Minnesota : Capstone Press, [2019] | Series: Fact
    finders. Amazing animal colonies
Identifiers: LCCN 2018029018 (print) | LCCN 2018035778 (ebook) | ISBN
    9781543555592 (eBook PDF) | ISBN 9781543555554 (hardcover) | ISBN
    9781543559125 (pbk.)
Subjects: LCSH: Termites—Juvenile literature. | Animal colonies—Juvenile
    literature.
Classification: LCC QL529 (ebook) | LCC QL529 .S74 2019 (print) | DDC
    595.7/36—dc23
LC record available at https://lccn.loc.gov/2018029018

Editorial Credits
Editor: Carrie Braulick Sheely
Designer: Ted Williams
Media Researcher: Heather Mauldin
Production specialist: Katy LaVigne

Photo Credits
Alamy: Premaphotos, 20 (bottom left), Thomas Cockrem, 21; Ardea Picture Library: Auscape, 15 (bottom); iStockphoto: Atelopus, 13, 16, Cheng_Wei, 19; Minden Pictures: Chien Lee, 7, 22, John Abbott, 10 (top right); Shutterstock: 7th Son Studio, cover (background), Andrzej Kubik, 10 (bottom left), CECIL BO DZWOWA, 27, ChaiyonS021, cover (bottom), 1, chakkrachai nicharat, cover (top), corlaffra, 28, Decha Thapanya, 24, Filipao Photography, 9, guentermanaus, 20 (top right), Kateryna Biatova, 11, masuti, 4, Randy Bjorklund, 15 (top), sarunrod, 17, sydeen, 15 (middle)

Printed and bound in the USA.
PA48

Table of Contents

CHAPTER ONE

THE ONE AND THE MANY

⬆ Many types of termites live in colonies underground. They dig tunnels through the dirt.

A termite digs a tunnel. It creeps along as it looks for food. Finally, it reaches a tree stump. The termite turns around and goes back to the **colony**. As it moves, it leaves a scent trail behind. Soon thousands of other marching termites follow the scent trail to the food. The hungry termites eat and eat. They head back to the colony. They digest the wood and poop. Young termites eat the poop. It has small **microbes** in it they will need when they grow up.

All for Colony Survival

Not all termite colonies are underground, but all are **superorganisms**. Each living thing is an organism. Termites and some other animals form superorganisms. Everything the individual colony members do keeps the colony alive.

AMAZING FACT
Sometimes a termite will even give up its life for the colony's survival.

colony—a large group of insects that live together
microbe—a tiny living thing too small to be seen without a microscope
superorganism—a group of living things that work together as a whole

Termite Teamwork

For termites, being part of a colony means living in a highly organized group. Different **castes** do different jobs. Scientists call the society in which termites live **eusocial**.

One of the most important jobs is taking care of the young. Only a few termites in a colony can have offspring. A caste of workers cares for the young. These workers do not have offspring of their own.

Colony life offers many advantages for termites. They share the work of gathering food and building a nest. Soldier termites protect the nest when it is attacked.

One problem is that most individuals can't live long on their own. They can do just one job. Without other termites for the other jobs, they die.

But the good parts of termite colony life outweigh the bad ones. Many termites acting as one can do things that no termite could do alone.

caste—a group within a colony that does a certain job
eusocial—living in a group in which usually one female and several males produce offspring and other members care for the whole group

Soldiers make up one termite caste. They protect the other colony members.

AMAZING FACT

Ants and some types of bees and wasps are also eusocial. Like termites, they live in organized colonies.

CHAPTER TWO

PAST AND PRESENT

Termites are a successful group of **insects**. They have been around for millions of years. Today they live on six of the seven continents of the world.

Ancient Termites

Termites have existed for at least 150 million years. In 1993 scientists wrote about a **fossil** termite nest found in Arizona's Petrified Forest National Park. They think it may be 220 million years old.

insect—a small animal with a hard outer shell, six legs, three body sections, and two antennae

fossil—the remains or traces of plants and animals that are preserved as rock

Termites branched out from a group of wood-eating cockroaches. These cockroaches lived in families. Termites may have been the first animals to live in organized colonies. Fossil termite bodies from 100 million years ago show that the termites belonged to different castes.

a termite fossil

Termite Types Today

Today there are about 2,900 **species** of termites. They fall into four types:

dampwood termites

- Dampwood species live in moist places. They build nests in damp or rotting logs, cut wood, tree stumps, and leaves.

- Drywood species live in dry wood. They nest in forest trees and in wood that has been used to make houses, fences, furniture, and boats. They live in more parts of the world than dampwood species.

- Subterranean species mainly nest in soil. Some build nests in trees or other places above ground. But they still dig for food underground.

termite mound

- Mound species live in dry areas. They build nests of hardened, dried earth. These usually look like hills or mounds on the ground. The nests can be several times taller than a grown person.

  species—a group of closely related organisms that can produce offspring

Around the World

Termites live on every continent except Antarctica. It is too cold for them there. There are no termites in the icy Arctic either.

The number of termite species is highest in the tropics. These warm places are near the Earth's equator. Mound-building termites are found only in the tropics and other warm regions.

North America

Europe

Asia

Africa

South America

Australia

□ where termites live

Antarctica

CHAPTER THREE

THE LIFE OF A TERMITE

A termite's body changes as it grows. Its final size and body type depend on two things. One is its species. The other is the role it will fill in its colony.

Queens, Kings, and Eggs

Termites hatch from eggs. A large female called the queen lays the eggs after mating with her male partner, the king. The queen and king are called reproductives because they produce young. Many colonies have one king and queen. In some species, colonies have multiple kings and queens. They live in rooms called royal cells.

Queens of some drywood species lay a few eggs each day. Queens of other species may lay tens of thousands of eggs a day. A few species produce 10 million eggs a year!

A queen grows much larger than the rest of the colony members.

AMAZING FACT

Most termites are less than 0.25 inch (0.6 centimeter) long. The largest are queens of the species *Macrotermes bellicosus*. They can be longer than 4 inches (10 cm).

Growing Up Termite

Nymphs hatch out of eggs. Nymphs look like tiny adults. A nymph sheds its skin, or molts, as it grows.

After several molts, each nymph becomes an adult worker termite. Some are workers forever. That is their caste. Others molt again. They become soldiers or reproductives. Reproductives are born with wings. They are called **alates**, which means "winged ones." Later, they shed their wings.

What makes a nymph become a certain caste? Chemical signals. Termites communicate through chemicals called **pheromones**. Other termites smell and taste these pheromones. The chemicals affect what termites do and how they develop. For example, the colony's chemical mix might signal that there are enough workers. Then more nymphs become soldiers.

The average worker termite lives one or two years. Queens live the longest. Depending on the species, they can live 10 to 15 years. A termite queen is among the longest-lived insects in the world.

alate—a winged insect of a species that has both winged and wingless members

pheromone—a chemical released by animals that causes other members of the species to change or behave in a certain way

The three castes of adult termites have different body types to go with their colony roles.

caste: worker

body type: may be smallest in colony, non-winged, no reproductive body parts

role: build and repair nest; gather food; feed young of other castes; clean eggs; groom other castes

caste: soldier

body type: large head, powerful jaws or other defensive feature; usually larger than workers; non-winged; no reproductive body parts

role: defend colony, especially king and queen

↑ queen termite

caste: reproductive

body type: winged when born; have reproductive body parts; queen is the largest termite in the colony

role: fly out of nest, mate, and form new colonies; replace the original queen and king if needed

A Queen and Her Clones

Termite queens in some species have two ways to produce offspring. A queen mates with a king and lays eggs. But as the queen gets older, she lays fewer eggs. She then makes extra queens to share her task. These extras are exact copies, or clones, of the original queen. They come from eggs that she produces without mating. This is called asexual reproduction.

The original queen still mates with her king. Her eggs become workers, soldiers, and alates. The new queens eventually replace the old queen when she dies.

↑ Workers care for all of a colony's queens and the eggs.

The Birth of a New Colony

Alates use their wings for mating flights. Many males and females leave the nest at the same time. They form pairs and mate. A pair then lands and finds a place to build a royal cell. They shed their wings. The new queen's first few eggs grow into workers. The workers build a nest and find food for the new colony members.

The king and queen continue to mate, and the queen lays more eggs. Once there are enough workers, nymphs become soldiers. In time, some nymphs become alates. They leave the nest to start new colonies.

TERMITE LIFE CYCLE

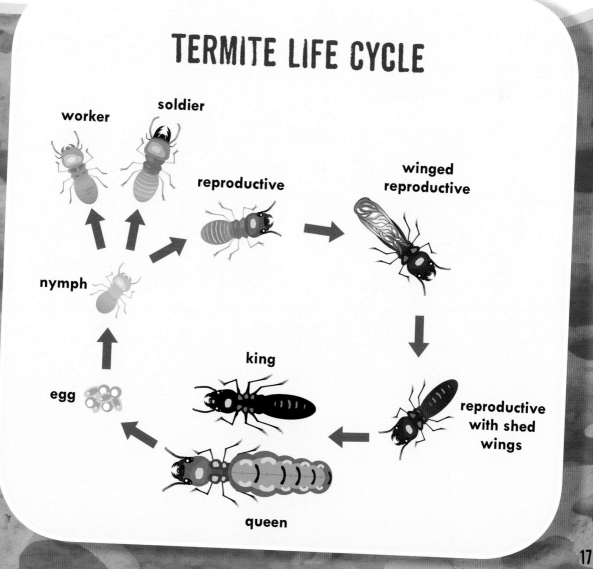

worker

soldier

reproductive

winged reproductive

nymph

reproductive with shed wings

egg

king

queen

CHAPTER FOUR

INSIDE A COLONY

Termite colonies may have a few hundred members or many millions. Whatever its size, a nest is a very busy place.

Building the Nest

When termites build a nest, each termite works alone. A complete structure comes from many termites doing simple jobs. The job of building never ends. If worker termites are not making their nest larger, they are cleaning and repairing it.

Drywood and dampwood termites chew through wood to make nests. Their nests have rooms on many levels. Tunnels link the rooms. Some rooms are nurseries for eggs or nymphs. Some are food storehouses. The termites may coat the walls with their waste droppings to form a hard surface.

Subterranean termites build underground nests. They tunnel through the ground with their jaws. Then they push the dirt out of the tunnels or pack it into walls. They also coat the walls with droppings.

Subterranean termites can build colonies that have thousands of members.

Some subterranean species build nests in trees. The nests are made of chewed-up plant material held together with droppings. These termites also make shelter tubes out of droppings. The narrow, covered passages often look like mud streaks. They connect the nest to the ground. When termites leave the tree nest to look for food underground, the tubes protect them.

⬆ a termite nest on a tree in Brazil

Mound-builders' nests are made of soil held together with droppings. They have two parts. One part is underground. It includes tunnels and rooms where termites live. The other part is the hill or tower above ground. The termites travel into the mound to repair it and defend the underground nest from attackers.

⬆ Many mounds of the Odontotermes obesus termite species stand in forests of India.

KEEPING IT COOL

Termites need air to survive. They must also avoid getting too hot. Mound-building termites' nests have tall, narrow towers that are open at the top. The mounds help move warm air out and cool air in. Scientists have several ideas about how this happens. One idea is that when a breeze passes over the towers, it pulls warm air up and out of the mound. Cooler air is drawn in through entrances and air holes closer to the ground. Another idea is that the change from hot days to cooler nights moves air in and out of the mound. This type of cooling structure is called a solar chimney.

The Eastgate Centre in Harare, Zimbabwe, has solar chimneys based on termite mounds. It uses one-tenth of the energy that would be needed to run electric air conditioners.

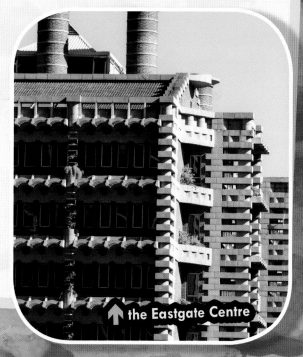

the Eastgate Centre

Workers transport food balls back to their colony.

Feeding the Colony

Workers gather all of the colony's food. Termites eat plant matter. Drywood species live almost entirely on wood. **Bacteria** and other small organisms in their guts let them digest wood. The young eat the poop of adults. The poop has microbes in that allow the young termites to eat wood as adults. Other termites eat leaves, grass, and farmers' crops. They may eat soil that contains bits of dead plants. Termites also eat animal droppings that contain plant matter.

A few termite species are farmers. They grow a fungus called *Termitomyces* in their nests. It grows on termite droppings full of hard-to-digest wood. The termites eat the fungus. Spores in their droppings then produce new fungi. The termites and the fungi need each other to survive.

Communication

Termites are expert communicators. But they don't communicate the way people do. Termites mostly communicate using pheromones. They also use touch.

Termites taste chemicals in the air, on the nest, and on one another. All termites can release chemical signals to mark trails. The markings say, "Follow me!" They help other termites know where to go. Each colony also has its own chemical blend. It lets nestmates recognize one another and their home.

bacteria—very small living things that exist everywhere in nature

AMAZING FACT

Scientists think that termites in East Africa were the first to become fungus farmers. It may have happened as early as 31 million years ago.

Termites also tap or stroke one another with their antennae. This can show that a termite wants to be fed or groomed or that it wants to feed or groom another.

War!

Soldiers are the colony's fighters. Ants and other insects often invade termite nests. Spiders, salamanders, anteaters, and birds also eat termites. Termite colonies also go to war against one another over food-hunting territory or nest sites.

A soldier guards worker termites.

When a nest is attacked, soldiers spring into action. Soldiers may use their heads to block tunnels. Some species squirt painful liquids at their enemies. Nasute soldier termites have nozzle-shaped heads. They spray a chemical that keeps attacking ants from coming too close. Some species have a gland in their bodies. The gland explodes when they are attacked. The explosion releases a sticky substance that traps the invaders. It also kills the termites. The termites die for the good of the colony.

WORKER DEFENDERS

In some species, soldiers aren't the only termites willing to sacrifice themselves for the colony. In 2012 scientists studied the *Neocapritermes taracua* species. These termites live in rain forests of French Guiana in South America. The scientists found that the workers in this species grow explosive sacks on their backs. The workers carry around a toxic blue liquid in these backpacks. The sacks grow as the workers age. When they are attacked, the sacks explode. The workers die, but the attackers die too. The oldest workers are more likely to explode their sacks. Their sacks are the largest and most toxic. Scientists believe these older workers are the least able to gather food. The explosive sacks help them be more useful to the colony.

CHAPTER FIVE

TERMITES AND PEOPLE

People and termites live near each other across much of the world. Termites are useful to people in some ways. They are a problem in other ways.

Termites for Food and Medicine

Insects are a food source in many parts of the world. A 2015 study found that more than 40 species of termites are used as food. People eat termites in Mexico and in parts of South America, Asia, and Africa.

In India, Brazil, and some African countries, people use termites to make traditional medicines. People who use these medicines believe they can treat certain illnesses. These illnesses include asthma and whooping cough.

AMAZING FACT

Do you like pineapple? That's what some people think raw termites taste like. Cooked termites are said to taste like nuts or vegetables.

A boy eats dried termites in Zimbabwe.

Termites as Pests

For some people, termites are pests. Termites can **infest** wooden structures. They damage buildings by eating the wood from the inside. Termites also feed on and ruin crops such as rice, sugarcane, coffee, and cotton. Each year termites cause as much as $30 billion worth of damage to buildings, trees, and crops in the United States.

Termites can help break down logs on a forest floor.

But termites help farmers too. Termite tunnels carry water underground. The tunnels keep heavy rains from washing soil away from the surface. Mound-building termites also improve soil. They move nutrients up from their tunnels to the surface.

Termites on the Clean-Up Crew

Have you ever wondered what happens to dead plants and wild animals or to animal waste? **Detritivores** eat all of this material. Without them, all of this waste would pile up. Detritivores include bacteria, worms, and crabs. Termites are also detritivores. They are very good at breaking down dead and dying wood. Scientists are studying organisms in termites' guts that use **hydrogen** and other gases to break down wood. Scientists hope the studies will lead to waste-disposal systems that turn plant waste into energy people can use.

Termites have been around for millions of years longer than humans. Although they can do damage, they also do important jobs that most people never notice.

infest —to spread in a harmful way

detritivore—an organism that feeds on dead and rotting material in nature

hydrogen—a colorless gas that is lighter than air and burns easily

Glossary

alate (AY-layt)—a winged insect of a species that has both winged and wingless members

bacteria (bak-TEER-ee-uh)—very small living things that exist everywhere in nature

caste (KAST)—a group within a colony that does a certain job

colony (KOL-uh-nee)—a large group of insects that live together

detritivore (di-TRY-tuh-vor)—an organism that feeds on dead and rotting material in nature

eusocial (yoo-SO-shuhl)—living in a group in which usually one female and several males produce offspring and other members care for the whole group

fossil (FAH-suhl)—the remains or traces of plants and animals that are preserved as rock

hydrogen (HYE-druh-juhn)—a colorless gas that is lighter than air and burns easily

infest (in-FEST)—to spread in a harmful way

insect (in-SEKT)—a small animal with a hard outer shell, six legs, three body sections, and two antennae

microbe (my-KROBE)—a tiny living thing too small to be seen without a microscope

pheromone (FER-uh-mone)—a chemical released by animals that causes other members of the species to behave in a certain way

species (SPEE-sheez)—a group of closely related organisms that can produce offspring

superorganism (soo-per-OR-ga-nism)—a group of living things that work together as a whole

Read More

Best, B. J. *A Termite's Colony.* Animal Homes. New York: Cavendish Square, 2018.

Harasymiw, Mark J. *Termites.* Animals of Mass Destruction. New York: Gareth Stevens Publishing, 2015.

Wheeler-Toppen, Jodi. *Orchid Mantises and Other Extreme Insect Adaptations.* Extreme Animal Adaptations. North Mankato, Minn.: Capstone, 2014.

Critical Thinking Questions

1. Name one type of termite nest. What parts of its design help the colony survive?
2. Name one of the main ways termites communicate. How is this similar to or different from the way insects that don't form colonies communicate? Use online or other resources to support your answer.
3. Do you think that termites do more good or more harm for people? Explain why.

Internet Sites

Use FactHound to find Internet sites related to this book.
Visit *www.facthound.com*
Just type in 9781543555554 and go.

Index